P9-DNF-169

Jeb Stuart

MILITARY LEADERS OF THE CIVIL WAR

Don McLeese

Rourke

Publishing LLC

Vero Beach, Florida 32964

www.rourkepublishing.com

PHOTO CREDITS: Title page and p27-National Park Service
P05 ©Getty Images
P10 Courtesy of Emory and Henry College
P19 National Archives and Records Administration
all other images from the Library of Congress

Title page: One of a thousand memorial statues to the dead and wounded at
Gettysburg National Military Park.

Editor: Frank Sloan

Cover and page design by Nicola Stratford

Library of Congress Cataloging-in-Publication Data

McLeese, Don.
  Jeb Stuart / Don McLeese.
      p. cm. -- (Military leaders of the civil war)
  Includes index.
  ISBN 1-59515-479-5 (hardcover)
  1. Stuart, Jeb, 1833-1864--Juvenile literature. 2. Generals--Confederate
States of America--Biography--Juvenile literature. 3. Confederate States of
America. Army--Biography--Juvenile literature. 4. United
States--History--Civil War, 1861-1865--Cavalry operations--Juvenile
literature. I. Title.
  E467.1.S9M25 2006
  973.7'3'092--dc22
                              2005010983

Printed in the USA

Rourke Publishing
1-800-394-7055
www.rourkepublishing.com
sales@rourkepublishing.com
Post Office Box 3328, Vero Beach, FL 32964

Table of Contents

~

J.E.B

~

James Ewell Brown Stuart was one of the greatest **generals** of the Southern **Confederate** Army. He wasn't known by his first name, James, but by the initials of his first three names, J.E.B. Many people thought "Jeb" was his real name!

He served under Robert E. Lee in the U. S. army before the Civil War started. When Lee became leader of the Confederate army, Stuart was one of his most important and trusted officers. He fought in many famous battles, including those at Bull Run, Chancellorsville, and Gettysburg.

Jeb Stuart became famous as the South's greatest **cavalry** officer. **Soldiers** who rode horses were called the cavalry.

Of all the officers on horseback, Stuart (at right) was considered the best.

*General George Washington shown during
the Revolutionary War Battle of Trenton*

Son of an Officer

~

Stuart was born on February 6, 1833, in Patrick County, Virginia. It seemed that he was born to be a soldier. His father, Archibald Stuart, had been an army officer during the War of 1812. Jeb's mother, Elizabeth, was the granddaughter of a soldier who was a hero during the Revolutionary War. From both his father and mother, Jeb learned that being an army officer was a great honor.

Revolutionary War and War of 1812: Both of these wars were fought against Great Britain. In the first war, which lasted from 1775 to 1783, the United States of America won its freedom from Britain and became its own country. Neither side won the war of 1812.

A Big Family

~

When the baby they named James was born to the Stuarts, they already had three girls and three boys. He was the seventh of the ten children they would have. He was the youngest son in the family, with three younger sisters. The family lived on a **plantation** named Laurel Hill.

The Stuart family was very religious. From his mother, Jeb learned to love going to church. Even after he became a famous officer in the Confederate army, soldiers knew that he was a man with a strong faith in Jesus Christ.

Plantations: The plantations in the South were often much bigger than the farms of the North.

8

Plantation owners often grew cotton on their land.

A modern photograph of the campus of Emory and Henry College

Off to College

~

A smart boy, Jeb was only 15 when he started college in 1848. He had learned a lot at home. He went to Emory and Henry College in Virginia until 1850. What he most wanted to do was become an officer in the army, like his father had been. In 1850, Jeb was selected to enter the U.S. **Military** Academy. He would continue his studies there, and he would also learn how to be a great leader in the army.

Military academies: The army, navy, and air force all have their own academies. These are colleges that prepare students to be military officers.

One of the Best

~

The U.S. Military Academy is in West Point, New York. Sometimes the school is just called "West Point." Everyone there was a good student, but Jeb was one of the best. Students there are considered part of the army. They are called **cadets**. There were 46 cadets in Jeb's class.

Jeb Stuart at the time he attended West Point

When he graduated, Jeb ranked 13th best out of those 46. He also earned the rank of cavalry sergeant when he graduated. This was the highest that a cadet could earn. Jeb was known to his fellow students as someone who worked hard and had a strong religious faith.

A view of West Point, which overlooks the Hudson River

Pioneers moved from the eastern United States to settle in the Midwest.

Taming the West

After Jeb graduated from West Point in 1854, the army sent him west, into the land that is now the state of Kansas. Some people known as **pioneers** were moving into this territory. People already living there, called "Native Americans" or "American Indians," had fights with those who wanted to settle there.

The Native Americans didn't want to give up the land where they'd lived. Jeb became known as an "Indian fighter," a soldier whose battles with the Indians helped make it safe for settlers to move there.

Kansas: Kansas became the 34th state in the country in January of 1861, a few weeks before the start of the Civil War.

Slavery Days

~

During the years that Jeb spent in the Kansas territory, Americans began arguing more and more about slavery. Slavery is when one person owns another person. A **slave** received no money for his work. Many slaves had been brought to America from Africa to work for free.

Most of the states in the North thought slavery was bad and should be made illegal. Many of the states in the South had slaves working on farms and plantations. Since Kansas would soon become a state, there were fights over whether it should be a "free" state (with no slaves) or a "slave" state.

A newspaper of the time sets forth the argument whether Kansas should be a free state or a slave state.

17

The attack on Harpers Ferry

Harpers Ferry

~

One man in Kansas who hated slavery was named John Brown. In 1859, he led an attack on Harpers Ferry, in what is now West Virginia.

John Brown wanted to get guns for slaves and to help them fight for their own freedom. Since this was against the law, the army sent Jeb Stuart to lead the fight against Brown. This was Jeb's most famous battle before the start of the Civil War. The army officer who sent him to Harpers Ferry was Robert E. Lee. He would soon become the leader of the Southern Confederate army.

John Brown: In 1855 and 1856, Brown led battles against men who were in favor of slavery, and he tried to help slaves escape. Some people who agreed that slavery was bad didn't agree with Brown's use of violence to stop it.

The War
Between the States

~

The Civil War lasted from 1861 until 1865. When the Northern (or Union) side won, the Southern (or Confederate) states returned to the United States.

When the Civil War started between the North and the South, Jeb left the U. S. Army and joined the Confederate army in 1861. His home state of Virginia had become one of the Confederate States of America. These were all Southern states, where slavery was legal.

People in the Northern states believed that slavery should be against the law. The United States said that the Southern states couldn't start their own country. The Civil War between North and South would decide whether the United States would be one country or two.

20

Stuart took part in the Battle of Antietam.

A Great General

~

Within the year, Jeb earned the rank of general in the Southern army. As a leader of soldiers on horseback, he fought bravely at the First and Second Battles of Bull Run.

When General Stonewall Jackson was wounded in 1863, Jeb became the leader of Jackson's troops at the famous battle of Chancellorsville. He was also the leader of the Virginia Cavalry Brigade. Stuart was brave and smart, leading his soldiers on horseback past the Northern army by going around it a couple of times instead of riding straight into battle.

Virginia Cavalry Brigade: The state of Virginia had its own company of horseback soldiers, led by Stonewall Jackson.

*Stuart's close friend
Stonewall Jackson*

22

After Stonewall Jackson was wounded,
Stuart took command of his troops.

A Very Colorful Soldier

~

It was easy to recognize General Stuart by his flashy uniform. He usually wore a cape with red lining, tied with a yellow ribbon. His hat had the huge feather of a peacock in it. This feather was called a **plume**. His soldiers would see him on horseback and would know to "follow the plume."

Stuart was easily identified by the plume in his hat.

The Battle of Gettysburg was a turning point in the Civil War.

Gettysburg

~

Jeb also fought at Gettysburg, one of the most famous battles won by the North. From July 1 to 3, 1863, the two armies battled near this small town in Pennsylvania. As he had done before, Jeb tried to take his **troops** around the enemy, while the leading Southern general, Robert E. Lee, attacked straight ahead. The Southern side had fewer soldiers than the North. Some said Jeb had made a mistake by trying to go around.

Jeb Stuart in a photograph taken during the Civil War

28

"Do Your Duty"

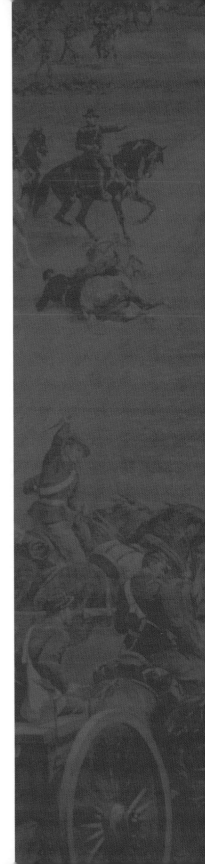

Jeb was only 31 years old when he died. He was shot by a U.S. soldier at the Battle of Richmond in Virginia. He told his soldiers to keep fighting. "Do your duty, as I have done mine," he said. One of the best and bravest of Southern generals, Jeb Stuart died on May 12, 1864.

Important Dates to Remember

1833   James Ewell Brown Stuart is born.

1848   Jeb starts college at Emory and Henry.

1850   Jeb enters the U.S. Military Academy.

1854   Jeb graduates from West Point and is sent west by the army.

1859   Jeb fights against John Brown at Harpers Ferry.

1861   Jeb joins the Confederate army when the Civil War starts.

1863   Jeb fights at the battle of Gettysburg.

1864   Jeb Stuart dies.

Glossary

cadets (kuh DETZ) — students at a military academy

cavalry (KAV ul ree) — soldiers who fight on horseback

Confederate (kon FED ur et) — a person, state, or soldier on the Southern side in the Civil War

generals (JEN ur ulz) — those with the highest rank in the military

military (MILL ih TARE ee) — the armed forces

pioneers (PIE uh neerz) — the first people to settle a land

plantation (plan TAY shun) — a large farm where workers live and crops are planted and grown

plume (PLOOM) — a large and colorful feather

slave (SLAYV) — a person owned by another person

soldiers (SOHL jerz) — people who serve in the military

troops (TRUUPS) — soldiers

Union (YOON yun) — the Northern side in the Civil War

Index

Further Reading

Davis, Burke. *Jeb Stuart,* Burford Books, 2000.
Greene, Meg. *James Ewell Brown Stuart* (Famous Figures of the Civil War Era), Chelsea House, 2001.
Johnson, Clint. *In the Footsteps of J.E.B. Stuart,* John F. Blair Publisher, 2003.

Websites To Visit

http://www.us-civilwar.com/jeb.htm
http://www.civilwarhistory.com/jeb.htm
http://en.wikipedia.org/wiki/JEB_Stuart

About The Author

Don McLeese is an associate professor of journalism at the University of Iowa. He has won many awards for his journalism, and his work has appeared in numerous newspapers and magazines. He has frequently contributed to the World Book Encyclopedia and has written many books for young readers. He lives with his wife and two daughters in West Des Moines, Iowa.